Listen:

A Black Woman's Journey to Liberation

Copyright © 2019 by Nirvana K.C.
Published by ZL Publishing House

Book Cover Design by Dionna Womack and Clinton J. Robinson Sr.

A CIP catalog record for this book is available from the Library of Congress.

Nirvana K.C.

 Listen/ by Nirvana K.C.

ISBN-13: 978-0-9992639-9-0 (ebook)
ISBN-13: 978-1-7339974-0-9 (paperback)

Made in the USA

10 9 8 7 6 5 4 3 2 1

Listen:

A Black Woman's Journey to Liberation

Nirvana K. C

PUBLISHING
HOUSE

Contents

Acknowledgments

Dedicated to Dallas Collins and Arthur Hill.

Prologue

The path that we walk is not our own. Our story has already been drawn out, every experience a divine purpose. Good or bad, these experiences mold us to whom we are destined to become. "Why me!" we so often yell out when turmoil, pain, and grief enter our lives. Alternatively, maybe the thoughts of self-hate, negativity, or insecurities flood our brain. As I took on my journey through life, I had to stop internalizing these defeating thoughts, and words, and I had to ask myself: "Where is this path taking me?" For a long time, I didn't know the answer to this question. My experiences throughout my life helped me answer this. The answer I came to was that my path was taking me to become a humble server. Not the servers that we see in the restaurants that pass out our dinner plates, but a server of the people. By realizing where my path was taking me, I viewed everything differently. I was no longer the angry bruised black girl being tossed around on this path asking why me, instead I accepted that the pain I have endured throughout my life could eventually help another young woman through her journey. I accepted things as they were and humbled myself in the experience.

In the good times, I laughed and savored the good moments. Remembering the happy times my family and I shared, the aromas of the food cooking on Christmas and Thanksgiving. Me being presented at our high school senior girl's banquet, followed by me walking the stage obtaining my diploma, and then later my degree. The feeling of accomplishment and pride filled my entire body. The joy of my wedding day, walking down the aisle, looking at the love of my life in front of me, this followed by the birth of my first born daughter, the love and eternal happiness I gained from her is beyond what I could have ever imagined. I absorbed these happy moments that surrounded me, and I analyzed how these moments contributed to my great divine purpose.

Just as I accepted the good times, I also had to learn how to accept the bad times. Thinking about the bad times can be painful. Thinking back to, the tears that ran down my face when I didn't feel like the dark-skinned girl looking back at me in the mirror was beautiful. Thinking back to, the agony my heart felt when my family betrayed it. Thinking back to, when I was sexually assaulted, knowing that from that moment I would never be the same. Thinking back to, the pain I endured of failed expectation when I worked tirelessly to be seen as an equal to white women, but American society only saw my dark-skin, not my attributes. Thinking back to, when my husband hurt me deeply. I longed to be in a loving marriage, but God had different plans for my life. Thinking back to, the moment I found out that my grandfather, my Paw Paw, was no longer in my life.

Each painful experience I have endured has molded me into the woman I am today. There were times that I felt that I was not going to make it. There was a moment in my life that I didn't want to live anymore. The bad moments seemed to outweigh the good moments. During this time in my life, I felt alone. Through this book, I don't want anyone who may be reading to think they are alone. My pain was my momentum to document these stories, in hopes to encourage another young woman.

Listen: A Black Woman's Journey to Liberation is a self-memoir about reclaiming control over my life, developing self-esteem, and finding a stronger sense of self-confidence. This book opens a window into my life in order to help others close their own. Each ACT has a collection of life experiences ranging from abuse, rape, betrayal, motherhood, and ultimately to how the journey led to liberation. ACT I begins my battle with self-image. It goes into intimate detail about my journey to love my skin-tone, hair, and weight. ACT II illustrates some of my early and later life traumas. It dives into the abuse I endured as a child along with the experience of facing an abusive partner. ACT III discusses the racial turmoil I encountered after moving from a predominantly black town to a predominately white town. Lastly, ACT IV explains the emotions of loneliness I felt growing up and now due to the separation of my family.

God allowed me to succumb to my lowest point so that He could build something greater, a testimony bigger than my life itself. It's a testimony that can reach across hearts, across the world. To whom may be reading my story, know that you can't give up. Trust me, God will lay out an Angelic landscape just for you. I write this to share my pain, but to also glorify God for my victory. This book is my Testimony.

Reader Survey

1. Are you:

   Single ☐   Married ☐   Divorced ☐
   Separated ☐   It's Complicated ☐ Dating ☐

   Check all that apply

2. On a scale of 1 – 10, with 10 being the most positive and 1 being the least positive, what role does either religion-faith-spirituality, if any, play in choosing a life partner? **Circle one.**

   1   2   3   4   5   6   7   8   9   10

3. What is your age range:

   18-25 ☐   26-34 ☐   35-44 ☐
            45-54 ☐   55+ ☐

4. Have you ever been in love? Yes ☐ No ☐ Maybe ☐

   If yes, please use one word to describe that feeling:

   _____

5. Have you ever had your heart broken?

   Yes ☐   No ☐   I Don't Know ☐

   If yes, please use one word to describe that feeling:

   _____

6. Have you ever been a victim of domestic violence?

   Yes ☐   No ☐   I Don't Know ☐

   If yes, please use one word to describe that feeling:

   _____

   The National Domestic Violence Hotline: 1-800-799-7233

7. Have you ever been a victim of sexual violence?

    Yes ☐   No ☐   I Don't Know ☐

    If yes, please use one word to describe that feeling:

    _____

    The National Sexual Violence Hotline: 1-800-656-4673

8. For each of the following statements, rate yourself on a scale of 1 to 10, with 10 being the most positive and 1 being the least positive. **Circle one.**

    I like the person who I am today.

    1   2   3   4   5   6   7   8   9   10

    I know precisely what I want in my life.

    1   2   3   4   5   6   7   8   9   10

    I am working to find myself.

    1   2   3   4   5   6   7   8   9   10

9. Write down five things you like about yourself. Write down five things you dislike about yourself.

    Five Things You Like about Yourself

    1. _____

    2. _____

    3. _____

    4. _____

    5. _____

Five Things You Dislike about Yourself

1. _____

2. _____

3. _____

4. _____

5. _____

10. Do you love yourself?

     Yes ☐   No ☐   I Don't Know ☐

ACT I:

Am I Beautiful?

Am I Beautiful?

"I cannot run away from who I am and my complexion or the larger society, and how they may view that."
~Lupita Nyong'o

As a young child leading up to a young adult, I battled with my self-esteem. I didn't truly comprehend my inner-beauty. I constantly compared myself to the images that I saw throughout the media and to others around me. The media depicted fair skin and long silky hair as beautiful. Since I was the only black girl in my class, I yearned to look like the other girls. I didn't feel beautiful in comparison to what I was exposed to on a daily basis.

One evening as I prepared to go to bed, I remember looking into my bathroom mirror. As I stood there my reflection gazed back at me: I was dark, from my head to my toes. The only white on my body was my teeth and the outer part of my eyes. My almond shaped, brown iris eyes, stared back at me. The hair, on the top of my head, felt thin and frail from years of perms and press.

Only in the fourth grade at the time, I would enter my homeroom class, and all I saw were white faces, I was the only black student in my class. I was trying so hard to fit in my new environment. My classmates would make fun of me, saying that my dark skin made me look dirty, "why are you so dark" they would ask me.

Slashes from fourth graders, their words replayed in my mind. I turned from the mirror and stepped in my bathtub. My small body barely took up half of the bathtub. I reached for my "skin lightening soap" and began to scrub—crying, scrubbing, swearing, scrubbing, and praying that God made me beautiful. "God, I wanted to be beautiful," I said aloud. "Make me beautiful!"

Thinking forward, as a young black woman in white America, you can't help but become brainwashed by the standards of beauty that are projected into our minds. Having fair skin, long straight, silky hair, and big blue eyes are advantageous to social positioning. These traits make you the typical "All-American girl," however what am I? Am I not beautiful? Am I not beautiful due to my hair being coiled into locks, framing my face, and my melanated skin? My eyes a dark brown, and my nose is big, all accompanied by full lips. Is this type of beauty worth being considered beautiful in mainstream America? Their standards of beauty are not me, and it will never be.

So how can I be beautiful if my skin is sun-kissed with darkness? How can I be beautiful if the hair that grows out of my head is thick and curly? The answer to this is within.

Looking back on that young child in the bathtub, my heart mourns her pain. I think, what would I say to her: "Baby girl, you're beautiful! God made you perfectly!" In addition, I would tell her that beauty is not a standard, there is no graph or measuring tool that can determine how beautiful one is. Beauty is found from within and projected to the world.

As I have gotten older, I have tried many things to change the way I looked in the eyes of others. I straightened my hair, put on makeup, and even changed how I spoke. However, none of those actions made me feel beautiful on the inside. The quest to find my beauty stretched across years until I turned twenty-two years old. During those early years, I endured life's pains. Moreover, I did everything in my power to feel beautiful. Even if that meant losing what made me beautiful on the inside.

Am I Beautiful to You?

"We need to reshape our own perception of how we view ourselves.
We have to step up as women and take the lead."
~ Beyonce' Knowles-Carter

As time passed, my appearance was a constant battle. Leading into my junior year of high school, I became obsessive over my weight and hair. I needed to have the latest hair weave installed. If I had to show my natural thick high shrinkage hair, I felt ugly. I stepped on the scale every morning to try and maintain my weight at 145 pounds. I felt like me being thin with long hair would make me more appealing. Unfortunately, even though I constantly put in the effort to maintain this idea of beauty, I was still ostracized in many circles.

I joined the dance team, and always ended up behind all the other girls. I knew I deserved to be up front, but I blamed myself for not looking like the other girls on the team. I was not petite. I had broad shoulders, big thighs, and large breast. I started to think that if I became the best if I worked hard and outshined everyone I would be in the front. Those thoughts resulted in me practicing tirelessly for hours every day. My kicks were higher, my leaps were wider, and I made sure to catch my baton every time it came down from being tossed in the air. I knew I became the best, but although I was the best, the standards of beauty still haunted me.

As I look back on the first day of the biggest crash diet I've ever done, it lasted two weeks. I lost 20 pounds. I wish someone could have told me the importance of individual beauty. The day before I began my two-week journey to lose weight, I attended one of the biggest tryouts of the year.

I closed my eyes anticipating the task I had before me. I imagined what it would be like to perform in this enormous stadium. I imagined the bleachers full of people, full of judgmental faces, but I wouldn't see them. All I would see are the lights. I wouldn't hear their judgmental words. I would hear the sound of the band blaring in the background. At that moment, I wasn't the fragile black girl everyone knew me to be. At that moment, I was a performer and artist. In that moment, I am fierce.

The only thing that weighed heavy on my mind was making the majorette team so that I could be a fierce force on the field. This try out was for the Cotton Bowl parade and game. In HBCU (Historical Black Colleges and Universities) SWAC bands, it was a moment to showcase who could put on the best field show. Bands from all across Texas prepared for this exciting event. Excitement ran through my entire body! I was ready. I knew the routine.

When my number was called from the roster, my heart leaped. I stood up from my spot in the lineup of dancers. I walked, owning every step. The try-out began as soon as I took that first step out onto the dance room floor. I walked to the middle of the floor. Four judges looked across at me. I took a deep breath, and the music starts.

5.6.7.8 and 1. That first move is the beginning to an energy filled performance. On the last beat, I hit my right split, smiling hard, baton in hand. Yes! I thought to myself the hard part is over. Applause rang out, and our instructors called over the girls that were going to perform, me being one of them. I thought the hard part was over, but I couldn't be more wrong.

Our male dance choreographer began to explain to us all of our requirements for attire and team "look." I was scheduled to get a hair weave sew-in so that my hair could extend down to the middle of my back, and I was to have on a "full face" of makeup on performance day. *This isn't too bad I thought to myself.* I began making a checklist in my head of all his requirements.

My instructor showed us the uniform. It was a leotard, the neckline plunged in the front and met where the fabric disappeared, and later met together to cover the bikini area. From the rib cage to the bikini line was all skin. My optimism quickly faded. Looking at the line of clothes, my thoughts began to blurt out self-doubt. "I would never look good in that," I thought to myself.

The cut was all wrong. I had natural bodily curves. My thighs would make the uniform look like I was prancing in nothing. I had a small stomach that would show through the open cut out in the uniform. My breast wouldn't even fit smoothly in the top of the outfit. My coach eventually walked up to me and said, "We are going to order yours three sizes smaller. If you want to dance, you have to fit in the uniform." I looked at him, and then my eyes shifted to the tiny piece of cloth he held. My head dropped immediately. "I got you," was my response to his demeaning expectation.

All of the girls in the room squealed of excitement about the uniform. They were shouting about "how cute," and "how fine" we were going to look in them. However, my mind was not filled with excitement. My mind was filled with defeat. I started to resent the other girls around me because my body wasn't going to look like theirs in the uniform. I loathed my fellow dancers, and I was infused with embarrassment and anger towards my dance instructor. Instead of excitement, my mind was focused on how I would lose twenty pounds in two weeks.

I started my weight loss journey the next morning. My feet are hitting the pavement, one after another, picking up speed as I thought about that little piece of cloth given to me by my male coach. The sun, burning my back, and sweat covering my face. I had every right to dance. I had every right to feel like I was included in a sacrificial group of exclusion. More importantly, I wanted to feel that I looked good by my coach's standards. I craved perfection, and I allowed him to set the expectation on my beauty.

Again, I lowered myself underneath societal pressures and even worse; I measured my beauty based on my male coach's standards of what he felt black women dancers should portray. I yearned to exceed my choreographer's societal standards, which didn't boost my self-esteem, but at the time I allowed myself to fall victim to the expectation. Weight had become an obsession. Building the perfect body had become a "life goal." The concerns of vanity and self-importance often engulfed the mind, body, and soul.

My instructor demanding we all fit into this sacrificial image speaks to his own image of black women. He didn't understand the dynamics of asking his all-black dance team to lose weight and install hair weaves. He didn't realize that his expectations were making us feel like we had to add to our being to become beautiful.

I Am My Beautiful.

"As you become more clear about who you really are, you'll be better able to decide what is best for you- the first time around."
~Oprah Winfrey

There were many times in my early years of life that I questioned the expectations of people. I didn't understand why so much was expected out of me. Although I didn't understand it, the lack of understanding didn't stop me from conforming to their expectations. Along with my battles, I faced with my skin color, and body, I toyed with an even deeper battle. I battled with knowing who I actually was. Not whom others wanted me to be, but who I actually was independent of others opinions and expectations.

Looking back on a day of realization, I was in high school. I stood in the dressing room that was connected to my bedroom and stared into my vanity mirror. The vanity lights illuminated my face, letting me see my reflection clearly. I was trying to see if the reflection look-ing back at me would change. Would my expression change into the selfish, scheming girl that manipulates everyone and gets her own way? Change into the girl that doesn't think of anyone but herself. The girl that doesn't care about people's feelings and what they think about her. Change into the "Perfect Replacement" as my momma describes me. Or maybe, it would change into a beautiful princess, the princess that gets her way, the one that roams her kingdom in the finest clothes, and looks down on everyone she passes. The one that nothing hurts her, she's so arrogant, and ignorant to notice the things that go on around her. She thinks things are perfect and never even glances at the big pic-ture if it doesn't feature her in it. Would my reflection change into the "Arrogant Princess," according to my brother? Maybe I would change into the good girl, the one that never thinks about boys. Just maybe my reflection would change into the girl that would finish college, and make something of herself. Change into the girl that devotes her time and life, to her education. The one that says "yes ma'am" and "no sir," the one that has it made, she knows what she will do in life, and the girl that never ever makes a mistake. Maybe I would change into the "Golden Child" according to the wishes of my grandparents.

The longer I stood there, facing my vanity mirror, staring at the reflection that looked back at me, I just saw me, as I perceived myself. I saw a teenage girl that had many questions. I saw a girl that tried so hard to do the right things. I saw a girl with so many flaws, a girl that hides her pain beneath a smile. I saw someone that tries to do so much for other people but gets tired sometimes. My perception was someone that yells when she's hurt, who cries when she feels pain, and who laughs when she is happy. I saw someone that loved her family dearly, but she hated where she was. I saw someone that loved her momma but hated the way she felt distant. My reflection showed a little girl that hated how her mother looked at her, she hated the way she had to cover up her tears, and she hated the way her pain seemed not to matter. She hated feeling like the bad person when she tried so hard but fell even harder. So as I freshened up, I saw a girl that sucked up the criticism, splashed water in her face to wash her tears away, put makeup on to cover the scars, and lip gloss to make the fake smile seem more real.

Looking back on this moment of realization I had, I realized that I spent so much time living up to different expectations. Trying to fit into the mold that family, society, and friends made for me. However, in all actuality, I am so much more complicated than a mold can hold. Looking back, I wish I had someone to tell me to not get caught up in others definition of you. The beauty of life is being able to define who you're without the influence of others. I needed to take a step back. Learn what I love, I needed to learn what made me cry, learn what made me laugh. Getting to know myself ultimately created the person I want to become. The mold that my family was trying to fit me in was not whom I was meant to be. I was not meant to be the perfect, "golden girl" or the "arrogant princess" not even the "perfect replacement." I was meant to walk a journey that would define me. When I learned to know myself and fall in love with myself, I attracted nothing but love.

I had to learn that no matter what other kids said about me, or what the expectation of my coach was, or even the expectations from my family, I would become what I build for myself. Beauty is not just the outer appearance it is your entire being. It is your spirit. It is your soul.

Change.

You make me want to change myself
Second, guess my beauty
Compare myself to pictures I know aren't real
Inject myself with poisons so I won't feel
Work long hours so I don't have time to think.
I ran from pain to get back into pain.
I battled with my image until I didn't look the same
Considered plastic surgery but had to realize that's insane
Push Ups till I was sore
Sit-ups until I can't do no more
Changing rearranging
Fixing what wasn't broken
Just so I can be your eye candy and gold token
Trying to buy sexy things
Humping and grinding acting like a sex Fein
Trying to keep you interested and invested.
You make me want to change myself
Cut off all my hair to look like the other bitch
Bought skin lightener because I saw you look at another bitch
Lit a blunt because I thought u liked that gutta bitch
Changed my strut cuz you said you liked them classy girls
Kept my smile because you didn't like it when I was mad
Made this false representation of me being glad
Took pill after pill to make me get smaller,
Stood up straight to make me feel taller
Punished myself with no food just water
And no I didn't stop there I went farther

Threw up once or twice how you think I lose that weight?

To fit into that dress on our lil date

You make me want to change myself.

Pile makeup on so I can be flawless

Staying in the mirror for hours so I can look good to you

Make you feel proud to say that's my boo

Took me a while to realize that the reflection looking back at me was beautiful

And that I had no reason to feel insecure.

Took me a while to say fuck you

And know I was beautiful for sure.

I'm not a Barbie doll that sits in a box

And I'm not that model girl that's on the tv screen

I'm not what society paints of me to be

I'm a self-proclaimed queen

And I'm beautiful with my locs and curls,"

I Didn't Know, I Was Beautiful.

"Are you the sweet invention of a lover's dream,
or are you really as wonderful as you seem."
~ Rodgers & Hammerstein's Cinderella

After graduation in my early twenties, I decided to make a commitment to my long time high school sweetheart. We began dating lightly in the tenth-grade of high school. He was a football player for my school's rival team. I was the Majorette captain. We saw each other frequently at football games. Although I rooted for my home team, whenever we played his school I hoped for his success. The summer going into tenth grade year, my crush invited me over for crawfish. I made up an excuse to take my grandmother's car and drove the three blocks to his street to visit. I met his entire family that day and filled up on crawfish and shrimp. We laughed and talked about our school rivalries and the upcoming game. Before leaving, we shared our first kiss. Looking back, he used the corniest line, and he looked at me as we sat on the couch. Right before I was about to head back home, he asked, "You know what I always wanted to do?" In tune with his thoughts, I answered "What?"

He then leaned in and placed his lips on mine. My entire body filled up with desire. I was shocked, it was the first time I had ever felt so much passion in my life. From that day we were inseparable.

Years passed, and we endured high school drama, cheating, self-esteem problems, trust issues, and family drama. We endured all of this, together.

By my sophomore year in college, I thought I had everything figured out. I was under the impression that I grew to love myself no matter what others thought of me. I fell in love with my physical self and accepted my shortcomings. I no longer lived up to the expectations of everyone else. Although very confident, I didn't realize how vulnerable I could be within a relationship. I never had an example, of a healthy union. My expectations were based on fictional stories like Cinderella. They were not based on true life circumstances, and I was not ready to endure the pain that a premature engagement had to offer. Although we both loved each other, we were still very young, and still maturing our relationship. I felt like we could mature together, not knowing at the time that we needed time to grow into ourselves individually. I didn't realize how dependent I was on him emotionally. Therefore when he proposed to me, I immediately said, "yes," not realizing where we both were in our life journeys.

The night of the proposal was hilariously perfect. I had a full-time management position in retail and didn't get off until very late. Therefore, the original Valentine plans were rearranged from a romantic evening at a jazz restaurant to a quaint dinner at IHOP. We sat and enjoyed the food while making small talk about our work day. I spoke about the annoyance of retail, and the boring meetings. I was so caught up in my story that I didn't even notice the diamond ring glistening in the light. I laughed out loud and asked him what he was doing. I looked at the ring and back up at him. He smiled and wiped a tear. He couldn't get the words out, but I already knew. "My knee hurts from falling from my longboard," he said as he smiled in my direction. Then another tear formed in his eye. He began his proposal, in between tears, and laughter. He stated that I was his gift from God and that he loved me and wanted to make me happy for the rest of our lives. I leaped from my seat, excited unsure, and emotional I gave him an enormous hug.

"Yes" I said. I was so delighted. I was going to be a Mrs! I was getting married to the man of my dreams! I was going to be able to commit to the man whom I have loved for the past five years. A man who has grown with me, learned with me, and fell in love with me. I was in love, proud, and excited to make the promise of a lifetime.

Following the engagement, we signed a lease for a small apartment in Huntsville. It was perfect for our lifestyle. It was up the street from my school, and down the street from his job. We made the little one bedroom apartment our home. We had donated furniture from our family members. The living room was filled with our black leather couches and a large T.V. I decorated the couches with pillows of our favorite colors. Red and purple lined the entire house. The outdated dining set that was given to us by my mother set underneath the dining room light adjacent to the kitchen that was decorated with purple Dollar Store towels on the stove, and red oven mitts, under the cooktop against the wall, held in place by thumbtacks. Almost two steps away was the small bedroom. His grandfather handcrafted our bed frame. The bed comforter was a mixture of red and purple. For the moment, our small apartment was made into our home.

Everything was perfect for us at the time but within a moment things changed. After one bad decision was made, everything began to spiral out of control.

On that day, my eyes brimmed with tears, and my heart wouldn't stop racing. The room began to spin. My mind was a whirlwind of emotions. As I read each text message on the phone messaging app, I grew more and more wearier. I started to pace the living room floor searching in my mind a solution. I felt stuck. There was no logical thought that came to mind. Our wedding announcements have been made. The venue has been chosen. Deposits have been made. Approval from my grandfather and father had taken place, and here I look at this phone screen in disbelief. I look at this phone screen, and then I see my life crumble around me. *"Five years. Five years. Five years."* These two words were ringing over and over in my head. He claimed he loved me. He claimed we would be together forever. There were no signs to warn me of this betrayal. We were both happy and thoroughly satisfied, so I thought.

My heart broke. I didn't know which thought hurt me the most, him going over there for merely sex, something he could have gotten before he left. Or, maybe it was that this girl didn't look anything like me. Or, it could be that we were on a path to a union and his actions showed me he wasn't ready or didn't want to get married.

I got up from my crouch on the floor. I ran to his new big screen TV. Do I break it? I turned and ran to my bottle of vodka. I drank all of it. With every swallow, I prayed it would knock me out. I wanted this all to be a dream. I didn't want this to be a part of my "perfect constructive reality."

I watched as the conversation unfolded before my eyes between her and him. He had just left our home, and now he was making plans to see another woman. I couldn't understand how he could betray me in this way. I read messages on the phone screen of the things they couldn't wait to do to each other. I read the messages of him saying he told me he would be out late with his friends. Every time he responded to her through the messaging app, I went deeper and deeper into rage.

I began to compare myself to her. Every insecurity I had battled from my childhood had resurfaced. She was skinny. She was a lighter brown compared to my dark skin. She had mixed curly hair in comparison to my thick tightly coiled hair. My thoughts became defeating. I said to myself, "you're not good enough, you're not pretty enough, and sexy enough." In general, I thought I wasn't enough. So, he cheated. I sat there with a bottle of vodka, and the wedding ring he placed on my finger now tossed across the room.

From the pain I endured from the betrayal of my fiancé going to have sex with another woman, I realized that I may have been too vulnerable to move past it in a healthy way. I realized that although his actions were hurtful, things got worse because I was not totally confident and secure with myself. Whenever one needs another person to make them feel "complete," or happy they needs to take time to be alone. Me making myself the problem shined light on my own insecurities. I was so threatened by the other women that I was ready and willing to change. I blamed myself for not being good enough. That was my first mistake. I forgot that I am not perfect and that my insecurities were normal. Everyone has those things that they would love to change, but one has to realize that flaws are what make them unique. I had to realize that my differences were not the problem. The fact that my skin was darker and my body had more curves than the other women didn't mean that I was the reason my relationship hit a brick wall. She had nothing to do with my fiancé's decision to betray our commitment to each other. I was better than the situation. I deserved more than feeling like I was even comparable to the other women. I needed someone to whisper in my ear at the time, "you're enough." I started to compare and try and outdo the other women. I needed to hear that competing was not the answer. I changed myself for a man that didn't see my worth. Changing myself didn't show my worth, but rather, shined light on how I felt about myself.

I realized that I craved to fix everything that went wrong, but I had to realize that I wasn't broken, and I wasn't in the wrong. I was beautiful before I cut my hair. I was beautiful before I lost the weight. I was beautiful before I changed my walk. After months of feeling betrayed and not "good enough," I was able to look in the mirror and see just how beautiful I was. I took the pain that my fiancé brought to me, and I changed it into my driving force to become better. I made sure I continued school; I stayed on my job and received two promotions earning me a Store manager position. Every time I felt my self-doubt creeping in, I reminded myself that I was beautiful and that I could make it without him.

Loving My Beautiful.

"I use to want you so bad, I'm so through with that.
Cause honestly you turned out to be the best thing I never had."
~Beyonce' Knowles-Carter

After my fiancé and I separated, knowing my worth and raising my confidence was an every day affirmation. I struggled, although I understood that I was not the problem, but I still had to adjust to him not being there.

One spring day after continually going through the motions of work, school, home, and then starting all over again the next day, I felt a weight being lifted. My room was dark. I kept it that way. I didn't want to have the sun shine through the windows because I felt so dark. I felt so dark for so long. But, this day was different. This day I woke up, and my heart didn't hurt. I didn't wake up with a tear-stained pillow. I woke up with energy, and dare I say, I woke up with a smile! A smile was on my face! I caught my reflection in the mirror, and I smiled larger. For the first time in weeks, I saw what my father told me about. I saw the beauty I never thought I had. I saw the sparkle that my grandfather told me about. I saw the glow my mother always said I had.

I got up from my bed and walked closer to the mirror. My face was clear. The little tummy that I had didn't seem that repulsing anymore. I pulled my hair back into a tight puff and put on a sundress. Seeing myself, dressed up made me feel even better. I ran out of my apartment. I ran into the sun. Feeling the warmth on my skin made me shout to God. I shouted because for the first time in my life, I looked at myself and didn't need anyone to say I love you. I was able to look at myself and love my damn self.

Throughout the hurt that I endured, up to this point I realized that a lot of my battle had to do with self-love. Loving oneself is the hardest journey because with love, one has to except the good and the bad. I had to know the worst of myself, and the greatest of myself, and accept it. By being in a long-term relationship at such a young age, I yearned for love from my partner. I became accustomed to him saying he loved me every day. My fiancé became my outlet; he became my cushion to the world. Although I loved him dearly, we parted ways. Not having anyone to show that love, pushed me to analyze myself. It pushed me to search for my own individualized happiness. Not the happiness I received with someone else, but my own happiness. It allowed me to capture love for myself, and happiness within myself. By doing, this I was able to forever be happy, my happiness was not in anyone else's hands but my own. I controlled my happiness, I controlled my love, and this gave me control over my destiny.

Through it all, I realized I am Beautiful, inside and out.

ACT I: Reflective Questions.

- *What are insecurities you have faced? How did you overcome them?*

_____

_____

_____

_____

_____

_____

_____

_____

_____

_____

_____

_____

_____

_____

_____

_____

_____

_____

_____

_____

_____

- *Have you ever compromised your self-worth?*

_____

_____

_____

_____

_____

_____

_____

_____

_____

_____

_____

_____

_____

_____

_____

_____

_____

_____

- *How has society molded your idea of beauty?*

_____

_____

_____

_____

_____

_____

_____

_____

_____

_____

_____

_____

_____

_____

_____

_____

_____

_____

_____

ACT II:

I'm Not Your

Enemy.

Big Girls Don't Cry.

Big Girls Don't Cry.

Keep ya head up,

Big girls don't cry,

Sit up straight,

Don't tell a lie,

No need to be shy,

Just let me have my way

It won't last all day,

A little touch here,

While I'm saying you're beautiful,

So full,

And youthful,

Wipe those tears girl,

Big girls don't cry,

It'll be alright,

Just don't tell anyone ya hear?

Or, you will feel more,

Feel more than just fear,

I'll take care of you,

No need to worry,

Your momma not home,

No need to hurry,

Ima take my time,

Boy, boy did I tell you, you was fine.

No, no don't scream now,

Get ya self together,

Big girls don't cry,

You wanna prance around,
And walk with guys,
Ima show you a real ride,
Why you covering up now?
No need to hide,
You hear that?
No one's here,
They won't hear the cries you making
Tonight you're for my taking,
Suck it up girl, Big girls don't cry.

The Enemy Creator.

"There is no greater agony than bearing an untold story inside of you." ~Maya Angelou

I was still very young, but I constantly dealt with trauma and emotions in a mature manner. The home I lived in was a place full of abuse, alcohol, and fear. My mother stayed in an abusive relationship for five years. The abuse she suffered trickled down to her children. I learned at a young age who was good, and who my enemy was. This particular day, my stepfather was my enemy, and his actions set the blueprint to how I emotionally connected with other people. He violated my trust and my feeling of safety.

As I reflect back on this day. I sat underneath the tree, breathing the fresh air, and trees surrounding me on all sides. I was unable to be seen, sheltered and hid from view. No one laid eyes on me; no one knew of where I could be. I liked it this way. I had a nice quiet spot that no one knew of but me. It gave me a sense of serenity and protection. It gave me ownership of my mind, body, and spirit. This was my place. My safe-haven. I loved the thought of "mine" it made me feel proud that something belonged to me after everything was taken from me. I was glad to still have my place. It was located in the back of the park, beyond the trees, near the pond out of sight. I was proud to call this place, "mine."

On this day, as the sun began to set, I could see that it was time for me to leave this cozy spot of mine and return home. I watched as the sky turned red, then purple, and then black as I walked down the long road back to the place I long to never return. A place that was not "mine."

"Open up!" I yelled banging on my outside house door. I wondered if they would hear me over the yells and banging of dishes. "Come on it's cold!" I yelled again banging my small fist onto the door. "What the hell you banging on my door for!" said my stepfather.

My step-father stumbled out of the house. The smell of beer reeked on his breath, and his eyes looked dreary and tired. I pushed passed him not wanting to look into his eyes. I tried to hurry to my room, but I was stopped as my body shook in fear. I saw my mother lying on the floor. I heard yelling, and someone was pulling my arm. Nothing mattered to me at that moment; nothing grabbed my attention as much as the puddle of blood near my mother's body, the tears streaming her face, and the cuts all across her body. She laid there watching me, watch her. She flinched when the tears came to my eyes.

"I'm sorry," she whispered; her lips barely audible. My mind went into a warp of events. I started to recant the happier times my mother, and I shared. I remembered when my mother would take me shopping. We would cook together, sing songs, and dance. In the culmination of our relationship she always taught me to be strong, and that a woman was the backbone of life. A woman had to endure so much more than a man. I didn't think she meant this.

Again someone pulled on my arm. This time harder and it yanked me out of my focus. I no longer saw my mom, but I saw a disappearing image of a lady lying on the floor as I was dragged in my room. I cried hysterically, not truly understanding what was happening. My step-father grabbed my arms and tightened his grip. He started to look at me up and down. He repeatedly told me how beautiful I was. I could tell by the look in his eyes that he desired the unthinkable. My brother stepped up behind him, as my stepfather was feeling up and down my arm before he could utter another word my older brother pressed his pocket knife in his back. "Touch her again, and I'll stab you."

I was left shaking in the room, terrified of being sexually violated. My brother exited my room after my step-father stormed out. I was left alone, shaking on the floor. I was afraid.

I was so angry that I would even be subjected to such abuse, and I was afraid of another encounter. I never felt safe in that house. Every time my stepfather came into my room I was afraid of his actions. Some days he would come in and rub my leg, speak to me for hours about how beautiful I was, and how nicely I was physically changing. Some days he would trash my room, ripping up my writings, and knocking over my clothes. Other days he would just beat my mother. I would hear her cries. The back and forth abuse causes me to question every act of affection because my idea of affection was misconstrued at a young age.

The acts of being sexually, physically, and mentally violated and abused extended past that present moment. To exacerbate the trauma, he indirectly assaulted my child, my sister, my friends, and everyone who was close to me.

The thought of something bad happening to my sister killed me. The thought of my sister one day telling me someone took advantage of her haunted me inside. I watched men look at us like adults when we were in the grocery store. I questioned hugs and kisses given by loved ones in our family. Everyone, and I repeat everyone, no matter who they were to me, I questioned them and their motives. This is what this constant cycle of abuse did to me. I couldn't look at anyone the same. No, you're not my friend. No, you're not my peer. You're a person on trial because from the moment I laid eyes on you, you entered into my judgment. You're guilty of the act until proven innocent.

Enemy You Are.

"There's an understanding of consent and respect that I think has gotten very confused in our culture..."
~ Tracee Ellis Ross

In college, I was re-exposed to the emotions of violation, and fear. My friends and I partied often. We would always have a good time, but on this day everyone went too far. I went above my alcohol tolerance. I knew of the dangers of allowing others to pour your drinks, but that night I wasn't thinking of what could happen. I was wrapped in the moment. I didn't notice when the guy I was laughing and speaking with put a substance into my drink.

"Cheers!" Everyone yelled. I was on my fourth shot. Four was my limit. Under the influence, the room was spinning, and my vision blurred. I can hear my roommate telling me something, but it was barely audible. I felt a tug on my arm.

"Come on and chill, you look drunk, haha!" My classmate pulled me onto the couch away from the others. The room started to spin out of control. I started to think back to how many shots we were downing. I looked across the room in hopes to see my roommate. She was nowhere to be found. I got up. He grabbed my hair to pull me back down. Seemed like the room was getting smaller. The noisy once crowded room seemed silent. I heard his breathing. I saw his eyes. He held me down, and I prayed.

He felt entitled, and felt because I couldn't say no that it was a yes. He felt that it was cool that he succeeded in penetrating the girl no one else could get.

After he removed himself from on top of me, I quickly exited the room.

I felt broken. I felt scared. Then I felt rage.

The thought of someone forcibly inserting themselves into me made me sick. For months I blamed myself. I constantly told myself if I didn't drink, or if I didn't even talk to him, the rape would have never happened. I beat myself down because I felt guilty. I didn't scream. I didn't kick. All I did was lay there and pray. I was disgusted with myself.

He Made Me His Enemy.

"Turn your wounds into wisdom." ~ Oprah Winfrey

I started to date again. I found myself acquainted with a tall, handsome musician. Everything about him peaked my interest. We took things slow. We went on dates and made music together. He seemed to have cherished the same values I possessed. After five months of us hanging out with mutual friends, he asked if I could help him out by letting him stay with me. Without giving it much thought, I opened my home to a guy I thought I knew. Over time, he grew more and more aggressive. He would drink excessively and blame me for any inconvenience he encountered. It took me almost losing my life to realize that the warning signs were my original clue to ask him to leave.

One night as I lay in my bed I heard the door open, and then slam shut. "Give me your keys," he yelled. He reached and snatched them out of my hands. Startled and scared, I jumped up from the bed and grabbed my phone. This rage was something new. He has yelled before but this time was different. His eyes. His eyes told me this was different. I wrapped my fingers around my phone and felt a hard pull. I fell backwards onto the bed. It was him. He began yanking my arm. The force was strong enough to make me lose grip of my phone. *"Oh hell no!"* This is all I thought. *"Oh no! This is not me! This is not going to happen to me!"*

I was yanked from one end of my apartment to the other. My head hit the wall, then the table, and then the floor. A ringing began in my head as my body crashed against the wall, the table, and the floor. What started his rage? When did it begin? I tried to get up, but he smacked my face. I got up again to run for the door, and he pulled me down. I hit the ground over ten times. He stood over me. His eyes were dark.

He looked so angry. In the moment, I started to think, what did I do? He began to walk to his gun. I bolted for the back door. He pulled on my arm, and I fought. He yelled. I ran.

There was a table on my porch. I was determined I wasn't going to fall again. That table was my savior. I threw the table at him, jumped my fence, and ran across the apartment complex. I had blood dripping down my face, but I didn't even feel it. My shirt ripped from my right shoulder down to the bottom hymn. My feet were bare, and nothing mattered at that moment. I needed to get as far away from him as possible. I kept running across the apartment buildings. The commotion was so loud people were already outside looking. "Do you want me to call the police?" A resident of the apartment asked. I looked up and calmly replied, "Yes."

This wasn't the first time he yelled at me. It wasn't the first time he snatched something out of my hand. It wasn't the first time he came to my job and degraded me in front of my co-workers. It wasn't the first time he used my money, my car, and my house and took advantage of my kindness. It wasn't the first time he lied. Just like in many abusive situations, it usually isn't the *first*. There are such signs. The signs are often subtle. I didn't think much of them.

I filled my mind with excuse after excuse. I told myself that he just needs love and understanding. I kept trying to tell myself this isn't as bad as I'm trying to make it. What I did was deny, deny. After he yelled, he always came and hugged me, told me I was special. He would kiss my hand, rub my feet, and dinner would await me. We would sleep, and the next morning the verbal abuse would begin. Abuse is a cycle. Unfortunately, many women go long periods of time before even realizing they are in an unhealthy relationship. Most of the time when they finally do realize, it's too late.

Each experience of violation took a piece of me. I battled with myself constantly searching for little pieces that these men took from me. I felt guilty. Each time thinking I could have did something to prevent what happened. When my step-father would enter my room, I use to think what if I just wasn't here. Would my mom have to fight so hard for nothing to happen to me? When I was raped in college, I blamed myself for not fighting back. When I was in an abusive relationship, I blamed myself for not noticing the signs. As the years passed, I grew beyond my feeling of guilt. I realized that I was a victim in these situations, and I should not allow them to define my journey and me.

I gathered my pieces and made myself whole again.

ACT II: Reflective Questions.

- *How have you overcome life-changing trauma?*

_____

_____

_____

_____

_____

_____

_____

_____

_____

_____

_____

_____

_____

_____

_____

_____

_____

_____

- *What are your "zero tolerance" standards in a relationship?*

_____

_____

_____

_____

_____

_____

_____

_____

_____

_____

_____

_____

_____

_____

_____

_____

_____

_____

- *Have you ever felt guilty after you have fallen victim to a situation?*

_____

_____

_____

_____

_____

_____

_____

_____

_____

_____

_____

_____

_____

_____

_____

_____

_____

_____

_____

ACT III:

Where Are the Black People?

I'm Black, Facing Forms of Racism.

"The most disrespected person in America is the black women.
The most unprotected person in America is the black women.
The most neglected person in America is the black women."
~Malcolm X

I remained in Huntsville after graduation, making my home away from home. The small town is known for the prison, but it is also filled with white people that just don't like blacks. My first experience of racism within the workplace was during my employment at a supercenter retail store.

Six hours into my work shift, and four more to go. I let out a sigh and started thinking of my dreams. I started thinking why I was at this store working my behind off overnight when the previous day was filled with lecture classes at the university. I stood in the aisle next to all the magazines, and tabloids, thinking of my dreams, finishing college, getting a new car, and publishing my book, all of which gave me a boost. I gathered the last bit of energy I had, walked around to the register, and began to greet the next guest.

"Hey, did you find everything okay?" I asked the young white male who was walking over to my register. He looked at me with my big smile showing, which I thought was very welcoming. But, instead of coming to my register, he turned all the way around and went two registers down from mine. I was not surprised that happened often.

I went back into my dream land. It was the place that helped me get through these last dragging hours. The distressed voice of our new cashier caught my attention. I looked up and I saw that she was having difficulties with the card reader. The guy that left my register was red faced at hers. He demanded her to slide his declined card again. I hurried from behind my register to lend a helping hand. I began to explain to him very calmly and in a professional manner that swiping his card too many times would cause his bank to flag the account, and as a result his card, will be locked. He looked at me and started to get even more outraged.

"What the hell do you know, lil' black girl?" Taken aback by his blunt racial hate, I just looked at him. He proceeded to slide his card again. This time it read declined, and it was locked. He went into a rage. "You dumb ass nigger, where is your manager?" he asked I was silent. "There must be a jail cell with my name on it because I have something for your ass!" he went on his words hit me. Every word he said. I knew that there were ignorant people in this world. Moreover, I've dealt with racism before. However, this was more than a dislike of black people. This was pure hate, and I felt it. He said he had something for me, and I believed him. His words embarrassed me. I felt embarrassed. I felt embarrassed to be black. Still silent, I stepped from behind the register grabbed my keys and left the store. As I walked out of the supercenter retail store, I couldn't help but feel enraged. The management team felt no obligation to de-escalate the situation. My respect was not considered a top priority. I later resigned. I realized no job or amount of money was worth the humiliation and hurt that the incident brought upon me.

I know that hate and racism are a part of this nation. It's something everyone will experience one way or another. Either one will be receiving or dishing out the racial hate. At that time, I didn't know my voice could be so useful. I folded in the time to stand up for myself, but then yet again why should I have to? Why should I even feel like I need to stand up for the right to be black?

Coming from a small black community, adjusting to the amount of hate that could reside in an individual was difficult. I was raised for the majority of my childhood in La Marque Texas. The town only inhabited about 16,000 people, the majority being minorities. I didn't understand the hatred. I didn't understand how a person that doesn't even know anything about me could hate me. Because I was a natu-rally soft-hearted person, that night, I cried. I not only cried because the guy hurt my feelings, but I cried for his ignorance. I cried for the community's ignorance. I cried because my manager said, "Get over it." I cried because the only person who didn't ask me, "What was the big deal?" was black. I cried because the man probably had children, and those children are going to be idiots.

Why does black equal ignorance to some in America? Why did he need to say "lil" before saying "black girl"? Why couldn't he just call me "ma'am." Everything he said was true other than me being little. I was far from that. So what bothered me? It wasn't the words. No, the words were not what bothered me. It was the feeling and emotion behind those words. For the first time in my life, I realized that I'm really not welcomed everywhere I go. I realized there are people out in the world that really hate me. Not because I did a bad deed, but because I'm black.

Black and In Charge.

"What would you do if you knew you were worthy?"
~India Arie

After leaving the supercenter retail store, I was able to acquire a position at a better retail store. I worked my way to store manager and started to truly realize what higher management meant in the context of leadership. Every day I worked with many different people, but I always knew that not everyone shared the same genuine hospitality that I did.

One afternoon I had a mother and daughter enter my store. The first impression was that she didn't approve of the fact that she walked into a black girls store. "Oh, you're the store manager?"

"Yes ma'am," I replied

"Oh okay, Ms. store manager. Get that down for me."

"Sure, what size can I get?"

"You should know what size, Ms. store manager. You should know what size I wear look at me."

"Well you look about a medium let me get that down for you."

"Ms. Store manager how much would this be with the discount?"

"Let me check." I reached for the top, which was hanging on one of our fixtures to double check the price. She pulled it back from me.

"You should know, Ms. Store manager? What's the price?" I looked at her and made sure my smile was bright as ever. This was her intention all along. She was waiting, waiting on me to mess up or to not know the answer to her question. I turned around and walked over to the register and began prepping her items.

"I been ready to go," she said as she slammed her items on the counter. "Thank you for your help though; you're a nice little black girl" her smile spread across her face, she was waiting, waiting on me to counter her blunt disrespect. I never gave her the attention she sought. She will not get that validation from me.

The very moment she walked into the store and placed her eyes on me, she had an agenda. Both she and her daughter were sporting Donald Trump stickers. Both women were frequent shoppers at our store, but black is not a common skin color you see running the store.

The last minutes of our interaction dragged on as I tried to keep myself calm. My thoughts became louder than her harsh piercing words. I kept reassuring myself that it will be over soon. I tuned her out, all of her sarcasm, and her looks. I focused on scanning her items and putting them in a bag.

Finally, she was gone. The uneasy feeling left. My second associate came into the store shortly after, and immediately noticed I was distraught. She asked what was wrong, and I could have shared this experience, but how can I explain being put down, being degraded, and how it was making me feel. How can I explain that the woman looked at me and judged me the second she walked in? How can I explain my experience of judgment and disrespect to a person whom this country was made for? She has never experienced this. What solid evidence did I have of her treating me in such a manner other than my *feelings*? Instead of explaining, I asked her if she could take over the floor. I needed a minute to take gather my emotions. My chest felt tight with anxiety and anger.

As a black woman in corporate America, I always felt as if I was on this constant climb to *prove* myself. I took countless beatings to my ego, self-esteem, and self-value, just to show that I was just as good as the other women of the other shade. I was always told by my biological father, as many other black children are often told, as a black person in America, you have to be "twice as good." As a black woman, I have to be twice as nice, twice as cute, twice as proper and twice as smart, because the moment a guest walks through my doors, they begin to judge. I become the negative black stereotype. There is that constant feeling, deep in my ego, that I have to overcome all of the known stereotypes of black women. Sadly, most people only know stereotypes, because the average majority citizen doesn't take the time to learn me past the stereotypes. To them, I will always be a "little black girl."

ACT III: Reflective Questions.

- *Have you ever felt like you had to prove yourself beyond the normal work conditions?*

_____

_____

_____

_____

_____

_____

_____

_____

_____

_____

_____

_____

_____

_____

_____

_____

_____

_____

- *How did you feel the first time you experienced racism?*

_____

_____

_____

_____

_____

_____

_____

_____

_____

_____

_____

_____

_____

_____

_____

_____

_____

_____

- *What does generational racism mean to you? How can it be stopped?*

_____

_____

_____

_____

_____

_____

_____

_____

_____

_____

_____

_____

_____

_____

_____

_____

_____

_____

_____

ACT IV:

I Stand Alone.

All Alone.

"A time to love, and a time to hate;
a time of war, and a time of peace."
~Ecclesiastes 3:8

The most painful feeling I have felt in my time being here is loneliness. After the pain of my childhood, transitioning to a young adult, I battled the feeling that no one was there to listen. I didn't think anyone understood my emotions. Looking back on a time when I was singled out of my immediate family, I was so young and very confused. I didn't understand why my mother and I had such a volatile relationship, or why my brothers and sister hated me. I was ostracized in my own home. I sheltered myself in my room every day. I stayed there day in and day out. I only spoke with my grandfather or grandmother. However, on this particular day, as I walked down the road from my high school to my grandparents three bedroom home where we all resided, I discovered just how alone I truly was.

I was having some "me" time, taking "my" time, taking each step slow, and steady. The walk from my high school to my grandparent's home was pleasant not too long, not too short. I meditated on each step. Thinking of the present kept me from going into my dark place. The place that as a 16-year-old, I thought no one could ever understand. Inside my head held a dark place that housed my emotions, my fears, and my anger. That place I just didn't want to go to today. I saw the street sign to my location. My steps became slower. I mentally prepared myself to enter this home of heavy negativity. Our home was filled with anger, hate, and resentment. My mother held anger towards me. She felt as if I was manipulative, and that I plotted to turn her parents against her. She convinced my siblings that I was against her, and them. They believed her; the misplaced hate festered in their hearts. My grandparents held sadness, seeing all their hard work being stolen from them. Items would come up missing, money, personal belongings, and they believed it was my mother. They mourned the loss of their once vibrant, honest child. I held resentment towards everyone. I wanted my mother to love and be proud of me, and I hated how my siblings blamed me for our situation. Our arguments took over the house during the day, and eerie silence would take over the night. We all would either be in a bed or laid out on the floor on top of blankets. No one spoke of the things that happened, and no one uttered a hint of the emotions we held inside. I stepped into the house and walked straight to my room. My goal was to block out all the negativity. I wanted to drown out all of the screams, the yells, and the crying.

My mother was going on her rant, cursing, and screaming at my grandmother. Yelling that no one understands her, she was justifying her hurtful actions. They were confronting each other about the family heirlooms that were stolen and sold, and about her leaving the burden of her children there and going to do whatever she desired.

It was normal behavior to me. I understood my mother was hurt, but I also knew that she needed to change. Her turmoil took over her once happy life. I tried to block it out, but how could I? I started to shut my eyes hoping that I could just drift asleep. Following the closing of my eyes, the walls shook. I jumped up and ran into my grandmother's room. My grandmother had a candleholder waving it at my mother. In response, my mother started pushing my grandmother back into the corner of her room. There was much anger, much hate, and much misunderstanding shown in both of their eyes. I lunged forward and grabbed my mother pulling her into the opposite direction of my grandmother. My goal was to separate them.

We struggled. My strength overcame my mother, and she flew down onto our wooden floor. My eyes widened. I didn't mean to throw her. Tears then began to fall. Before I could help her up, my younger brother attacked. He grabbed me by the neck and tightened his grip. I couldn't breathe. I was choking. My mom started to scream, "You chose her over me!" The events started to run past my eyes. I was losing air. My grandmother was yelling and crying. My grandfather, who could barely walk, was trying to kick my mother out of the house. I fought my brother. The only sounds for those thirty minutes were crying, yelling, and cursing. My family was at war. We had lost the battle of love that bonds families together.

Looking back on that day brings tears to my eyes. This was a true demonstration of how the Devil can destroy a home. The anger and resentment boiled over until we were all separated. We were all alone, trapped in our own anger and perception of each other. Again, my family was at war. We were battling each other. We were fighting blindly over individual battles never won.

We each internalized our emotions, selfishly ignoring the other person. Anger and hate outweighed our love for each other. Our problem was anger, and not knowing how to forgive. Along with the different demons' that road the backs of us all, the demon of jealousy, the demon of drugs, the demon of manipulation, and the demon of greed, were tearing my family apart. Sometimes things happen that we do not understand. I was singled-out by my mother. She blamed me for everything at that moment. I was the reason her family was torn apart. My brothers thought I intentionally hurt my mother. They were angry and wanted to let that be known. I didn't know how to counter what was happening. I didn't understand how so much anger could be directed to one person. I felt alone. My mother and brothers turned their back on me. But in a way, we all gave in to the demons of that particular day.

Get This Out.

As I sit and try to make sense of this world that I live in today.
Make sense, of why things aren't going my desired way.
Make sense of all these feelings I'm feeling inside,
It's driving me crazy,
Because these feelings, these feelings that I feel aren't right.
These feelings…
There unscripted,
Unedited,
Destructive,
There crazy.
These feelings their crazy,
They have no breaks, they are not lazy,
They constantly pull at my heart,
Constantly,
Constantly.….
Constantly,
Until I feel like my heart will stop beating…
Like, this is the death of me,
I cannot understand the feelings that I'm feeling that is within me .
Help me out,
Help me understand,
Help me understand why I feel the way I do!
Help me understand why I can't even love,
I can't even love the one I thought I would always love
The one I thought I could always cherish,
I knew,
I just knew our love would never perish.

I knew that you would always be there for me

And I knew that I would always be there for you,

But look,

At us,

This is all,

Brand new,

I do not understand

The feelings that I have for you.

Because it is not love,

It is almost hate,

But it cannot be called hate

Because I still relate.

I still relate to the love we had,

In the beginning of time.

I just wish we could rewind.

I wish I could rewind to the beginning of time when I loved you.

When I was in love with you.

Rewind to that innocent love,

When all I could do is look up to you,

I would see the love in your eyes,

Your eyes ran deeper than the skies,

I thought you were the truth.

But then you lied.

You lied

You lied

And.

You lied.

And I cried.

I became torn,

I became worn,
I entertained multiple men,
Wondering who would fill the void inside.
But if truth be told…
If truth was to be told.
The void was myself because I didn't know nor understand,
My own worth.
As I sit,
As I sit and try to get these words out,
These words to express myself,
I must relate to myself,
I must not disgrace myself.
Now as I enter the most trying time of my life,
I lost my grandfather,
I lost him .
He was weighed down by sorrow, and grief.
He didn't forgive, we didn't make things right,
The lies were in the dark, nothing came to light.
I know now he is in God's hands,
But he can no longer hold my hand.
I can no longer hear his voice.
I lost him.
and I selfishly hurt,
it's a pain I feel day and night.
But…
There is so much more.
More reasons to my heart being torn.
Its tore from my constant abuse from my youth.
Its torn from me not knowing were that line was,

The line that should not have been crossed , the line that left a little black girl lost.

Its torn from my momma not knowing how to be a momma, and my daddy not seeing the truth.

I have this hurt in my heart because I'm a gatekeeper

I'm a gatekeeper of a family that's torn.

A gatekeeper of a family that's dying,

They don't believe in second chances

They don't believe in trying.

My heart is torn,

Because I try to reach out my helping hand

And again, and again,

I get defeated,

I get mistreated.

And now I'm left with this hole where my heart used to be.

I'm trying to find that heart, because I know this heartless girl, that's floating around

In this heartless world, is just not me.

I understand that this heart. This heart is no longer there.

I need it to come back,

I need you to come back

Heart I need you to come back!

Because without you, I am not me,

Without you I cannot see,

I cannot see the good in the world that God wants me to see.

Heart come back to me!

Come back , so I can continuously love

I can continuously help

I can continuously be all that I am worth .

And I can live up to my wealth.

Heart come back to me.

I have disgraced myself, I have displaced myself

I'm rolling with the wrong crowd

People I know I have no business with.

There is so much drama in my head I cannot begin,

To dismiss.

I'm craving this attention that I think will help me out.

But really my mind is in a drought, I'm loss

I do not know where I'm going,

I'm blind,

I'm walking this dark tunnel,

Under this dark land, in this dark time .

All the way until the end of time asking,

God!

God!

God! Where are you!

Keep helping me!

Grab me, hold me, keep me,

Be my keeper, because as I look in the mirror…

I have lost all my features.

I have lost everything that made me, me.

I have lost everything that God made me to be.

I have gave it up to this world,

This world.

Why?

Why have I given it up to this world.

Its because I'm hurt.

And it's so unreal,

It is unreal because I know my body needs to heal.
But unfortunately the healing, is nowhere to be found.
It is gone, it is lost,
I went over to my love it was not there,
I asked my momma to please help me,
She just yelled and the comfort was not there.
I asked my lover, to please hold me and be there for me,
But unfortunately it was only the sex, mentally he was not there.
No one was there

I Stand Alone.

"Whoever dwells in the shelter of the Most High will rest in the shadow of the almighty." ~Psalm 91:1

Standing alone was the best thing to get away from all the extra noise. It allowed me time to get advice and healing from the universe and God. HE wasn't going to speak to me when I was surrounded by noise. One of my favorite things to do was walk the trails at the park on a quiet day. No kids to hear crying, and no stray dogs to run up to me. It was just the sound of my foot to dirt. The sound of the birds singing, the sound of trees dancing, and if I'm lucky, I hear the sound of peace. This is when I believe God is telling me that everything will be okay.

I Felt Alone.

"Know this, if someone has cheated on you who truly loves you, they have hurt themselves as much as they have hurt you."
~Jada Pinkett Smith

One thing that made me feel small, insignificant, worthless, and lonely, was that I loved a man that didn't know how to love me. Being in a relationship, all I wanted to do is feel loved. My second heartbreak with my high school love came around about three years later after we reunited. I reopened parts of myself that I held near to me, the parts that made up the core of me and made me most vulnerable. During this time I had grown emotionally, but still didn't fully understand how to guard my heart. I fell deeply in love again. We decided to pick up where we left off and get married.

My second heartbreak hurt worse than the first, it left me feeling isolated, and alone. Even though he was constantly around trying to "fix" his betrayal to me, I felt trapped. This time around I was expecting our first child. I felt as if couldn't leave.

Depressed and alone, I had few I could reach out to. The love of my life laid with my best friend. The day after our honeymoon trip, I received a phone call. My friend's voice was muffled in between tears. Me being worried and anxious, I just wanted to make sure she was okay. I asked her repeatedly what's wrong. Then in the background, I could hear her boyfriend at the time yell, "Tell her!" It seemed as if his words jogged an emotion inside of me that I already knew. I quickly hung up. I didn't want to hear the words from her.

My hand shook as I laid the phone by my side, and walked to the bedroom where my husband sat. "You have something to tell me, and you better tell it to me right." He looked up puzzled and asked what I was speaking of. My voice began to shake, and my knees felt as if they were going to give out. I took in another deep breath so that I could speak clearly. "If she tells me before you do, it will be far worse." His eyes immediately glossed over, and he began to cry. He looked at me and said, "you weren't supposed to find out, it was one time." Anger engulfed my body. I turned from him and ran out of the house to my car. My brain was showing flashes of all the special times we all shared. The birthdays, the birth of her children, my wedding day, and the whole time, they held this secret from me. I inserted the key in the ignition and started the car. My husband ran out of the house shortly behind me. He was out of breath, and his words were straight to the point, "you leaving?" He asked. "I don't know, but I have to get away from you at the moment," I responded. I backed my Toyota Corolla out of the driveway and sped off.

Learning this shortly after our wedding sent me into a dark place. I didn't know whom to trust, so I didn't talk to anyone. The emotions of the pregnancy, along with the loss of my "love high" and my friendship tore through me. Every day I stayed inside trying to make sense of it all. I knew it wasn't my fault. This time I didn't compare myself to the other woman. I knew that there was no comparison. But, it still didn't ease the feeling of betrayal.

Hell No Girl.

How am I supposed to hush?

Hush when I've seen silence

How can I hold my tongue

And you keep talking

Then I'm in the wrong because I get fed up

Fed up

We argue because I can't hold my tongue

Smh

Pitiful

I'm a bad wife I'm selfish because I left my home to be with a man and we argue just for my needs

My needs

I just wanna scream sometimes because I think I cannot be a wife

I cannot be a wife because you keep silencing me

You keep thinking I will abide by you

I will submit to you

But I will not let you disrespect me

I will not let you take me as your lesser

I'm not wife material

I felt that love is enough

But wife's gotta be yes girls

I say yes once or twice

Hell on a good day everything might go your way

But when you cross me

hurt me

cut me

touch me

I'm not your yes girl

I'm

Your hell no girl

Your, you got the wrong one girl

The fuck you girl

The how dare you girl

I don't like fighting

When I could have it all

I cater to you

By me being your wife I have catered to you

I have catered to you

You call me selfish

You call me bitch

I guess I'm selfish

I guess I'm the bitch

I guess you are always right

I guess I'm always wrong

I guess

I've never been right so this ain't new

How dare I

How dare I except being your wife.

I'm. Not wife material

I will never be your yes girl that ain't me

I guess I'm sinning against the Bible

I ain't gonna let you run over me

And you don't even see your wrong doings

So I take full responsibility

Full responsibility of you thinking you can. Silence me

Talk to me any type of way

Constrict me so I can not speak
because you were done
I take full responsibility
It's on me
It's on me that I can not argue back when I feel that you got it all wrong .
It's on me that I can not yell
That I can not feel
That I can't stand to be misunderstood
Or disrespected
It's on me
I ain't the good wife
But you knew this before you met me
You knew this before you kissed me
Before we made this life inside of me
You knew this before you said I do to me
You knew this so baby the only thing
The only thing that is your fault
Is marrying a selfish hell no girl.

I Should Have Stayed Alone.

"Being a woman, you deserve heaven and earth." ~ Kelly Rowland

The betrayal led to arguments that would last hours. We would yell and I would cry, every time I would mourn the loss of my love that I had for my husband, and I cried because I lost someone I called a friend. No matter the situation, it spiraled back to his lies, and his betrayal.

As I reflect back on the day I had enough. On this day, I let the words that we fought so hard to never utter escape my lips. My head was ringing as I'm holding my stomach crying. It hurts. I look down at my panties. They are red with blood. I kneeled down on the floor hoping I can calm down. I thought to myself, *"I can't lose my baby, not to this."* My body stopped shaking, the blood stopped streaming. I held onto the sink and started towards the door. I twisted the knob and opened the door to see my husband. I said, "Just leave it alone." I didn't care to tell him of the blood. I just needed to lie down. But of course, our arguments were never that easy to walk away from. "You're always running! You never talk! You just wanna run away!" He yelled behind me. "Aw, what's wrong with Barbie? Is Barbie mad?" he said in a patronizing voice.

"You never understand, please leave it alone!" I yelled, with the same motion I tried to slam the bedroom door. He barged through.

We argued for hours, by the end of the fight we didn't even know why it began. This was our normal. I couldn't take it.

"I want a divorce." The words came through my lips. "I'm so tired."

Stand Alone.

"Love is an endless act of forgiveness. Forgiveness is me giving up the right to hurt you for hurting me."
~Beyonce' Knowles-Carter

I knew of the statistics to explain why most marriages eventually come to an end. I just didn't want to be another statistic. There are ways to defeat the odds, but the fact is that the odds still remain. Acceptance, forgiveness, and self-love are to me what holds a marriage together.

Learning to accept the past could better prepare me for the present and future. A lot of times I held on to so much anger. Deep rage, because I never accepted what actually happened in my relationship. I may have said I understood, but the fact was I went to a different place, mentally. I would see my love, and when he leaned in for a kiss, I would think about something else, anything else to not let me soak in the deceit that has happened before me. Disassociating became the drug of the year. I never actually looked at him and accepted "okay" you betrayed me. "Okay" I forgive you. I didn't formally accept either state of mind so that I could move on. That never happened. Therefore, the acceptance didn't allow me to even begin to start the second process, which is forgiveness.

Forgiveness was hard, of course. Everyone says, "oh it's not that big of a deal," "get over it," and "move on," but I didn't think like that. It could have been my fault to hold on to grudges that tightly, but I was hurt, broken, confused and betrayed. I didn't know my first step. I never understood the first step. Having to accept that my friend and love held a secret from me was too hard, me accepting this pain was me accepting the mindset that maybe I made the wrong decision, it's me accepting the fact that my trust is broken forever. Who really wants to accept that? Forgiveness although important, and the core principle of marriage, this step I never crossed.

Eyes.

Looking into his eyes.
Waiting, hoping, he's looking into mine
Can you see me?
Can you see my eyes baby,
Can you see the light, so dim
So dim the light
Can you see the pain
Can you see it?
The longer you refuse to see me
The longer you refuse to see my eyes
Each moment that passes, you risk
Losing me.
Each moment that passes, my eyes
My eyes they trail further and further away.
From every harsh word
And every disagreement ,
Every tear you miss,
It snatches the light.
Oh baby please,
Don't miss this dim light
Because pretty soon
It will be to late
And that light
Will be gone,
And so will I
In the night.

Stand Alone Continued.

"It is better to be alone than to become a person that loses his soul to the fear of loneliness."
~ Shannon L. Alder

Some months passed, my husband and I were officially separated. He had decided to move to another state for a while, and I worked to gather the pieces of myself. The weight of being a single-mother sank in one day as I laid on my grandmother's bed. My baby girl was bouncing in my grandmother's arms. I stared at her. Inside I smiled because I knew I was blessed. But at that moment, I had so many emotions going on in my mind. I held back the tears as they glossed over my eyes. This little girl is all that I have, and although that is more than enough, what can I offer her? I was overwhelmed.

My phone never rang with a person telling me you're hired! My phone never rang with my husband either. He went on and experienced things he wanted to see, and I was alone. He was able to laugh, and make new good memories, while I cried not being able to get over the past.

I stared at my creation, she was literally the only thing that kept me on earth. I couldn't fight back my tears any longer. My suicidal thoughts made me enraged. They were selfish. I became mad at myself for even thinking that way, but how can I change it? I longed for support from the man I loved and hated equally. I wanted him to walk through the door and instead of making an excuse, or acting like everything was 'ok' I wanted him to look into my eyes and see I needed him this time, more than ever.

I was allowing my situation to break me. I fought in and out of depression because I could not get my "happy ever after" out of my brain. I was so hurt from the betrayal that took place. It consumed me. All I saw day in and day out were lies. My self-worth and better mind was at war with my heart. I came too far at this point in my life to revert back to nothing but pain. I had to accept my situation, and at the time I couldn't.

Self-love can be seen as a shield against acceptance and forgiveness. My self-love is what caused me to feel so much anger towards anyone who wronged me. Because I couldn't fathom allowing something to happen to me, it opened a portal of something deeper. I was no longer trying to accept and forgive his actions. I was trying to fight myself. I was trying to accept and forgive myself. Loving yourself and hating yourself at the same time is a torture that can drive the Devil into an eternal personal Hell.

Can't Breathe.

I can't breathe

The enemy got me by the neck.

Grasp getting tighter and tighter,

I can't breathe, words on repeat.

Rewind once, rewind twice

Our life is becoming a game of chance,

Like rolling dice.

Scoring the snake eyes, filled with lies.

And, we as a people shutting out our own cries.

Can't educate the black brotha and sista when we to concerned about reality TV and Trash ass Rap

Talking about money "get money" when we have blood being created in our streets like honey in the bees ghetto.

Money cannot be created if you dead. And how can you talk the hustle when every night you fed?

When nothing seems to be speaking the facts. Just portraying our race with a bruised face

When we gonna stop killing one another

The bullet now taking over

I shouldn't have to fear for my life

Every time I see a cop car I look over my shoulder.

The world just looks more cruel as I get older.

And the fools living in it makes the hot days seem colder.

The young kids walking around saying they hood.

Walking around the hood concept misunderstood.

The only good thing that's gonna come out of the hood is you in a box made of wood,

Stop perpetrating! Repping what you don't know, just for show.

How many tears are going to be tattooed on America's face until we realize our fate.

There needs to be a refocus on what's important.

There needs to be the genocide of race as a concept

And education needs to become a necessity

That's the only thing that makes sense to me

A mother waking up to a message saying her son dead

Don't make sense to me

Guys walking down the street waving guns in the air then get mad when it goes off don't make sense to me

Girls emphasis on vanity and not an education don't make sense to me

Girls changing their bodies to look like a bad bitch

A female dog they aspire to be don't make sense to me.

I'm choking on the ignorance this nation shows.

Every step I take it feel like it's life's tolls.

We Leave Alone.

"You think our lives are cheap, and easy to be wasted. As history repeats, so foul you can taste it."
~Lauryn Hill

There was a funeral on Monday, Tuesday, and Friday. Three burials were in one week. My phone rang, and my best friend was asking me what dish I was going to bring. All I saw was red this whole month. It seemed like there were more funerals than birthdays, more funerals than graduations, and more funerals than house parties. We got full at the funeral repasses, and not the dinners. A tear fell onto the floor as I put on a brave voice. I just wanted to be strong for his close friends and family, but the thought of how he died weighed down heavily on my heart. Senseless deaths! He didn't have to go, not this way. It wasn't his time. "I'll bring peach cobbler," I responded, and hung up.

My classmate was young, smart and funny. We shared many laughs, and I yelled at him once or twice for hurting my home girl's feelings. He was a father, a friend, a brother, and a son. I remember the day my phone lit up with a text, and it read he died. My heart immediately dropped, and all I could remember thinking was that he was just playing basketball the other day? It all felt so surreal. I didn't believe it until I saw him lying lifeless in the casket.

The day of the first funeral arrived. My hand trembled as I looked for my friend. I felt his pain in my heart and it crippled me. I spotted him, sitting with the family. He was a pallbearer. My eyes began to overflow with tears, as I got closer to the casket. My dear classmate looked so pale. I looked only for a second. I turned to my friend who was sitting in the second row of seats and hugged him tightly. "I got you," were my words. The only words I could utter out. I rose up and saw the mother of his child. I saw his child. She looked up at me our eyes met, and her pain shot through me. The same look in her eyes that everyone seemed to have. There was a look of disbelief, a look of tragedy, and a look of heartbreak. More tears streamed as I walked to my seat. I sat and listened as the preacher prayed. Eyes open. I guess that day I questioned my faith.

My high school class was very small. We all knew each other; many of us grew up side by side all through our grade years. It just seemed like that year my classmates, and I lost so many of our men to violence. Growing up in a project, or a small-town can be like a prison. Because in that small town, one falls victim to small-town problems, small-town gangs, and are alleviated with small town solutions. It's like the saying of crabs in a barrel. No one escapes—physically and mentally.

Always know that there is always a way out. If you want it bad enough, you can overcome the worst of the worst situations. We all are not born with a spoon in our mouths and our beds made of feathers. Sometimes we have to sleep on something hard to motivate us to search for better. You're not a product of your environment.

He Left Me Alone.

"Never take a wooden nickel." ~Arthur Hill

I was pacing back and forth in my living room. I had a small place, but it was my own. I inhaled slowly taking in the aroma of my lavender candle, trying to calm my nerves. My anxiety was on the edge, it was making my mind frantic, I was unable to focus. My heart was racing. My vision was blurry. Tears gathered in my eyes but didn't fall onto my cheeks. Back and forth, one foot after another, and my steps seemed to mimic my heartbeat. I didn't know what was wrong. I didn't know what my heart was tugging on. I decided to call my grandpa.

The phone rings. "Hello" my mother's voice was on the other end, not Paw Paw who I expected to hear on the other end of the phone.

"Hey! Let me talk to Paw Paw." I tried to sound happy, I wanted to make him smile because that always made me smile.

"Paw Paw isn't feeling well."

"What? Do I need to drive down there tonight? Is he really bad?" My heart was heavy, heavier than before.

"No you don't need to drive down here, he will see you tomorrow, but here he is," A moment later my grandfather picked up the phone, his voice was so weak, so dim. But he still answered the phone in his joyful dialect.

"HELLO!" Even though his voice was soft, it still sounded like my Paw Paw.

"Hey Paw Paw, I'm done with the song I wrote to you! I will sing it to you as soon as I see you tomorrow! I love you so much! Talk to you soon!" I could tell he smiled through the phone, this reassured me that he was okay.

"Love you," he responded

"Talk to you later," that time I didn't say bye. I'm not sure why I just didn't want to say bye.

The sun shined through the window, I sprang up, brushing my teeth getting ready for a short day at work then heading to see my Paw Paw. I called to hear his voice before going into work. Again, my mom answered. "Hey give the phone to Paw Paw!" I spoke into the phone. I was happy because I was ready to hear his voice and let him know I was coming to see him.

"Paw Paw isn't with us anymore" my mom's voice small and distant on the phone. After those words, I just buckled. I didn't even bother saying anything else to her. At that moment, I spoke to God. "No!" I yelled out my phone went across the room, I fell to my hands, then my knees, then somehow I was flat tears streaming, shaking uncontrollably. "No,no,no,no," is all I could say aloud. In my mind, I repeated, "*I was supposed to sing to you today, you were supposed to hear your song today.*" I cried and cried, from that moment until the sun went down. He was gone. My Paw Paw. My rock was gone. Never have I felt that alone.

My grandpa was a great man. He was like a dad to me. He was wise and hard working. He used to take me to go bike riding, we had picnics in the park, we flew kites together. He made life an experience. Every morning when we lived with him he made sure my brother and I had a full breakfast, with milk and orange juice. Not leaving until we finished every bite. I would always sit at the table longer because I hated drinking milk, but Paw Paw insisted on me finishing that darn milk. He stood up for me when no one else would. And he instilled in me values that I could never forget. He was very particular about honesty. He would look in my eyes and know if they were truthful. "You can lie to yourself, but not to me," he told me once. He taught me to work hard, and stay smart. "Never take a wooden nickel," he would say. Arthur Hill was and still is the best Paw Paw a girl could have asked for. Every night I still end my prayers with "I love you, Paw Paw."

ACT IV: Reflective Questions.

- *Have you ever truly forgiven another human being? How did you achieve forgiveness?*

_____

_____

_____

_____

_____

_____

_____

_____

_____

_____

_____

_____

_____

_____

_____

_____

_____

_____

- *How do you cope with death?*

_____

_____

_____

_____

_____

_____

_____

_____

_____

_____

_____

_____

_____

_____

_____

_____

_____

_____

- *What steps have you taken to guard your heart?*

_____

_____

_____

_____

_____

_____

_____

_____

_____

_____

_____

_____

_____

_____

_____

_____

_____

_____

Post-Script:
A Letter to My Daughter.

Dear Ava Londyn Davis,

My sweet girl, you're truly your mother's angel. I didn't think I could have you. The doctors said there was a chance you wouldn't make it. I smile every time I see your brown almond eyes because we proved them wrong! I want you to always remember you're a fighter. There are many things that this world is going to throw at you, but always know God always has the final word.

I have endured a lot, and I hope you can read this and learn that no matter what you can make it through. Even though I cried and I was physically and mentally hurt, each experience made me stronger, better, and wiser. Life isn't easy, but you control your own destiny. Ava, don't ever fall victim to tragedy. There are many things that may happen that are out of your control. There are many things in this world that you will not understand. Mommy wants you to know that that's okay. You can't control everything. And sometimes the answer isn't always black and white.

Ava, you taught me the true meaning of unconditional love. Because of you, I am able to show love. I realized that life is a gift, because God gave me you. You don't have to live up to what society paints as beautiful. Know that you're beautiful inside and out. Always know that you should never compromise your self-worth. Know your worth.

If you're ever hurt, get down on your knees and pray. There were many things I endured through life that my peers couldn't help me through. I looked around for others, but there healing didn't touch my soul. God was all I had left. If you ever find yourself questioning life, go to a quiet place, close your eyes and visualize God. You have a purpose.

Ask Him to reveal it to you. Let your purpose be your momentum to keep going.

Soon you will be a young woman. Every decision you make will not be perfect. Cherish the good experiences, and learn from the painful ones. Life is about learning. Seize every moment you have to expand your mind, spirit, and soul. Whether you experience your first heartbreak, or you fall in love, or you hit a brick wall or you achieve everything you want to, know that everything is temporary.

There will be a time that I am no longer with you physically. When that time comes, I want you to know you're still never alone.

Love, your Mother

Epilogue.

"My mission in life is not merely to survive but to thrive;
and to do so with passion, some compassion,
some humor, and some style."
~Maya Angelou

As I have journeyed through my life, I realized that every experience was a chance for me to grow into a better version of myself. With this collection of stories, I seek to encourage other people who may be reading this book to tell their own truths. There were a lot of things I didn't know about life, and still to this day I do not know, but I have learned to grow from the trauma, and I refuse to let it emotionally break me.

The difference in the girl at the beginning of this book and now, is that I am open to love myself. I am open to make mistakes, and I am open to judgment. I hope my experiences spark conversation. And as a result, we as human beings can sit and listen and learn from each other.

Self Reflection.

_____

_____

_____

_____

_____

_____

_____

_____

_____

_____

_____

_____

_____

_____

_____

_____

_____

_____

_____

www.ingramcontent.com/pod-product-compliance
Lightning Source LLC
Chambersburg PA
CBHW071947100426
42736CB00042B/2305